The Saint-Saëns Cello Concerto No. 1 Study Book

Volume Two

"Movement" Three

Concerto No. 1, Op. 33 by Camille Saint-Saëns
Exercises by Cassia Harvey

CHP350

www.charveypublications.com - print books
www.learnstrings.com - downloadable books and chamber music

The Saint-Saëns Cello Concerto No. 1 Study Book, Volume Two

Table of Contents

*Note: Measures not included in the table of contents are rests in the cello part.

About the Book

This book divides the last 281 measures of *Concerto No. 1 in A minor*, by Camille Saint-Saëns, into short sections and provides exercises for mastering each section.

The exercises are written to benefit both the professional and the student.

Each exercise was written to teach a specific section of the piece. **Shifts** are often taught with different notes in between to help establish a concrete sense of distance; muscle memory that can be consistently relied upon. **Double stops** are included for establishing relative pitch and building left-hand strength. Double stops with open strings are included to help the player develop and maintain good intonation.

Vibrato should be used throughout the book as soon as intonation is secure. Playing the exercises with vibrato will help balance the hand over the notes being played and will also help develop tone. Occasionally, reminders to use vibrato are included over the notes. These are not exclusive to the notes they are referring to; vibrato should be used in the exercises whenever it would be used in the actual *Concerto*.

Interpretation

These exercises deliberately do not teach interpretation or style. They were written to develop a secure and reliable technique that will free the cellist to explore a variety of interpretations and develop their own. Cellists can use these exercises to both learn the piece and maintain their technique for repeated performances.

Beyond learning to play the notes, cellists might listen to and critique other performances, deciding what they like in terms of style and expression. They might also learn about Saint-Saëns and the context in which the piece was written. But most of all, they should play the piece repeatedly, listening to and refining their phrasing so that their performances clearly reflect their own musicality and ideas.

Notes on Technique

Bowings and Fingerings

Unless otherwise marked, begin each exercise on a down bow (⊓).

If you change the bowings or fingerings in a section of the *Concerto*, go ahead and change the related bowings and fingerings in the exercises. The bowings and fingerings in the exercises should be as close to those used in performance as possible.

When two different fingerings are included (as in measures 440-451,) pick the fingering that you prefer and only play the section of exercises that support that fingering.

Tempos

Some of the exercises were written with slower note values than the *Concerto* so that the piece can be learned at a slower pace. These exercises can be played with increasing physical speed, eventually reaching the performance tempo.

Extending

The term *extend* as used in the exercises refers to an extended or stretched hand position. The traditional method of extending is to reach a whole step with first and second fingers so that the hand can span two whole steps. In the higher positions, *extend* may simply refer to reaching one note higher or lower than the fingers would otherwise reach in the traditional position. The term *closed* refers to the usual cello hand position that spans one whole step and one half step.

Accents

Accents in exercises are used to simulate urgency in the left hand as it relates to shifting. While shifts are most accurate when first practiced slowly, they must subsequently be practiced in the style in which they will be performed. Accents help the hand shift faster in exercises, thus preparing for the actual shift in the piece.

Strings

Strings are indicated by Roman numerals under the notes.
I=A string, II=D string, III=G string, IV=C string

Note: The last "movement" of the Concerto (from letter J
to the end) is broken up into sections in this study book.
The complete "movement" is at the back of the book.

Concerto
Section Seventeen: Measures 391-399

Concerto No. 1, by Camille Saint-Saëns
Exercises by Cassia Harvey

Learning the Notes
Measures 391-392

Note: More exercises for these notes are found in Volume One, beginning at page 21.

Agility
Measures 391-394

Rhythm I
Measures 391-392

Rhythm II
Measures 391-392

Rhythm III
Measures 391-392

Octave Shift
Measure 395

Agility
Measures 395-396

Shifting I
Measures 397-399

Shifting II
Measures 397-399

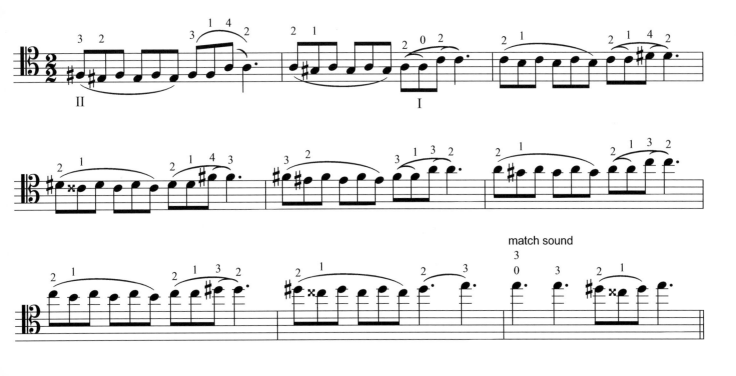

Shifting III
Measures 397-399

Note: The first two measures on each
line have only half step shifts.

Hearing the Intervals in Different Octaves
Measures 397-399

Shifting Duet for Ear Training
Measures 397-399

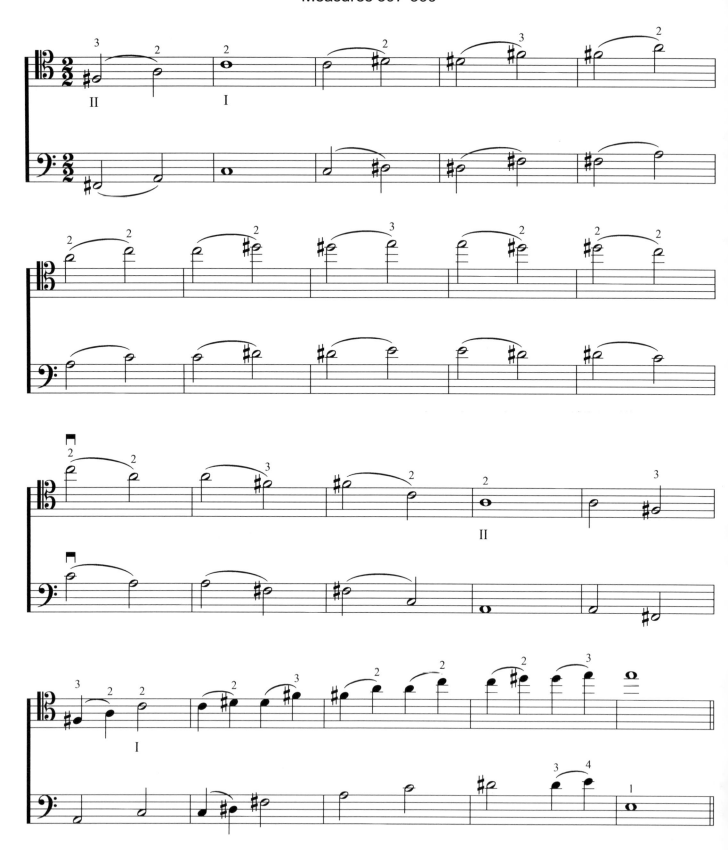

Shifting into each Position
Measures 397-399

Shifting between Positions
Measures 397-399

Mapping the Run: Measures 397-399

**Repeat this exercise several
times, playing faster each time.**

Rhythmic Shifting
Measures 397-399

Agility
Measures 397-399

Fluent Shifting
Measures 397-399

Finger Exercise I: Measures 397-399

Finger Exercise II: Measures 397-399

Concerto
Section Eighteen: Measures 407-436

Vibrato and Bow Control
Measures 407-411

Shifting I
Measure 412

Shifting II
Measures 412-413

Shifting
Measures 414-416

Shifting Overview
Measures 413-417

Rhythm
Measures 412-417

Shifting
Measures 418-420

Learning the Notes
Measures 418-425

Shifting Fluently
Measures 418-425

Learning the Notes I
Measures 425-428

Learning the Notes II
Measures 428-431

Learning the Notes III
Measures 432-434

Learning the Notes IV
Measures 432-436

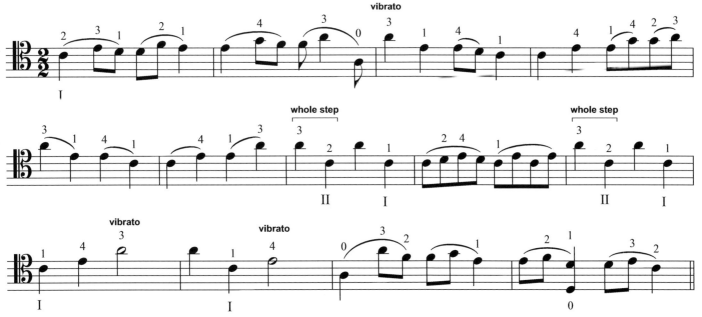

Shifting I
Measures 434-436

Shifting II
Measures 432-436

Concerto
Section Nineteen, Fingering No. 1: Measures 440-451

Learning the Notes I: Measure 440

Learning the Notes II
Measure 440

Note: In this exercise, only
the half steps are marked.

Repeat this section several
times, playing faster each time.

Learning the Notes III
Measure 440-441

match sound

Repeat this section several
times, playing faster each time.

Shifting to First Finger I
Measure 441

Shifting to First Finger II
Measure 441

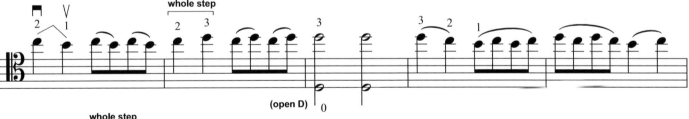

Shifting Backwards: Measure 441

Agility I
Measures 441-442

Repeat this exercise several
times, playing faster each time.

Agility II
Measure 441

Repeat each section several times, playing faster each time.

Speed
Measure 441

Repeat this exercise several times, playing faster each time.

Speed and Agility I
Measures 440-441

half step

Repeat this section several
times, playing faster each time.

Repeat this section several
times, playing faster each time.

Speed and Agility II
Measure 440-444

Repeat this exercise several
times, playing faster each time.

Speed and Agility III
Measure 440-444

**Repeat this exercise several
times, playing faster each time.**

Transitions
Measures 440-444

Please note: this exercise is deliberately awkward. It does not have fingerings that are typical in cello playing but rather mirror the fingerings in the piece. When played as fast as possible, this can increase fluency in the excerpt.

Shifting Back to 2nd Finger: Measure 441

half step

Shifting into Higher Positions I: Measure 441

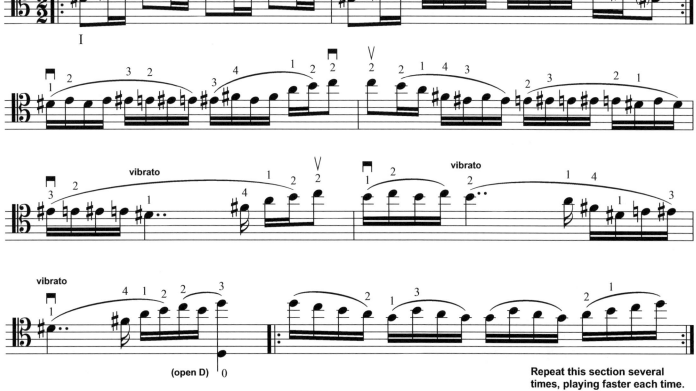

(open D)

Repeat this section several
times, playing faster each time.

Speed and Agility IV: Measures 440-444

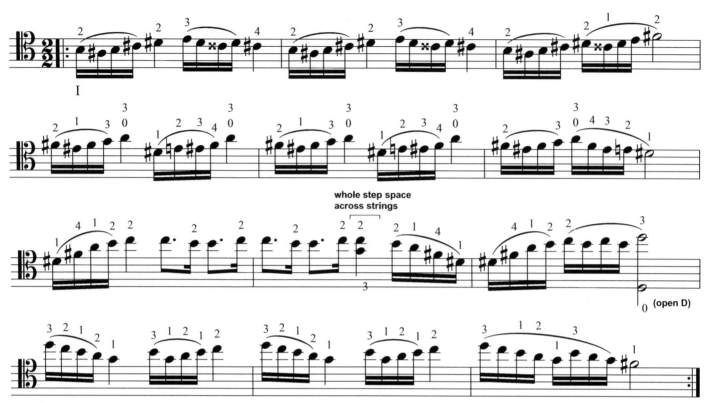

Repeat this exercise several
times, playing faster each time.

Shifting into Higher Positions II: Measure 441

More Transitions: Measures 442-443

Fluency
Measure 440-443

Repeat this exercise several times, playing faster each time.

Learning the Notes I
Measure 448

half step   half step

whole step   whole step

half step   half step

whole step

half step   half step   half step

Learning the Notes II
Measure 448-449

Double Stops for Strength and Intonation
Measure 448-449

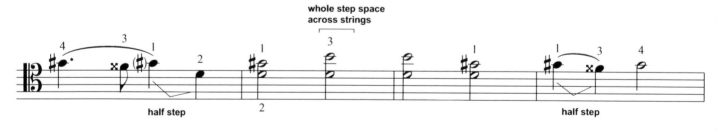

Fluency
Measure 448

Speed
Measure 448

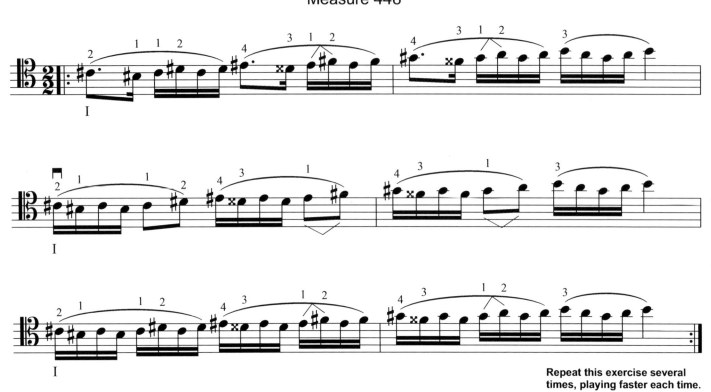

Repeat this exercise several times, playing faster each time.

Learning the Notes: Measure 449

Agility I: Measure 449

Agility II: Measure 449

**Repeat this section several
times, playing faster each time.**

Learning the Rest of the Notes: Measure 449

Shifting I: Measure 449

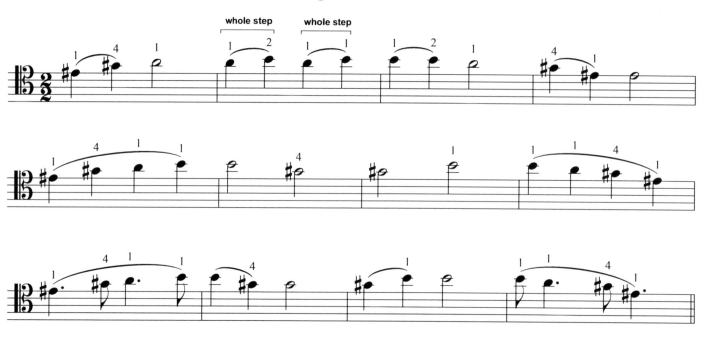

Shifting II: Measure 449

Agility: Measure 449

Learning the Notes Coming Down
Measures 449-450

Shifting Backwards
Measure 449

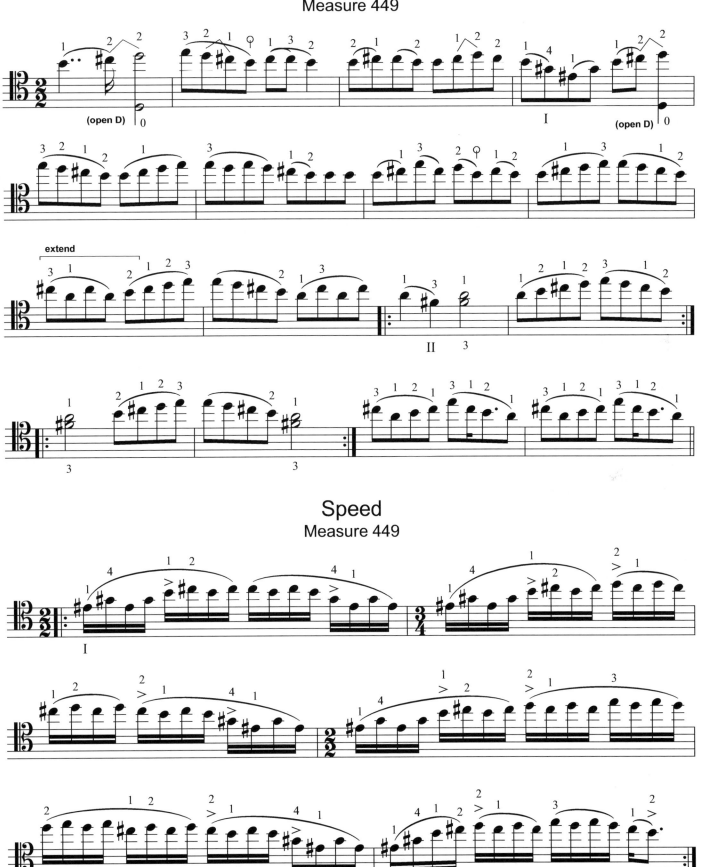

Speed
Measure 449

Repeat this exercise several times, playing faster each time.

Repeat each section several times, playing faster each time.

Speed and Agility I
Measure 449

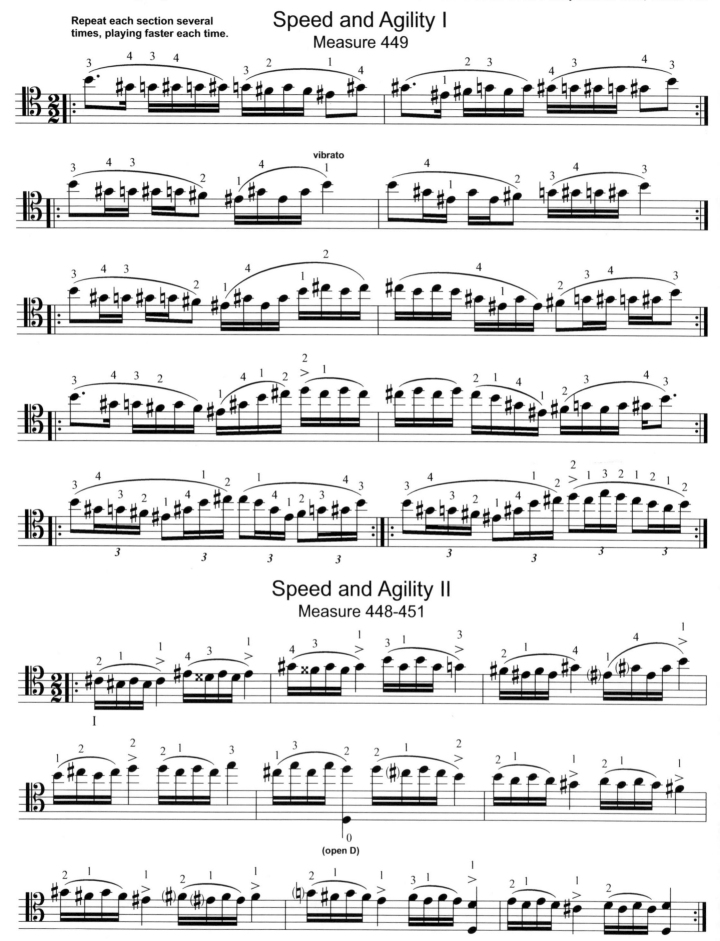

Speed and Agility II
Measure 448-451

Repeat this exercise several times, playing faster each time.

Speed and Agility III
Measure 448-451

(open D)

Repeat this exercise several
times, playing faster each time.

Shifting Back to 2nd Finger: Measure 449

Shifting into Higher Positions: Measure 449

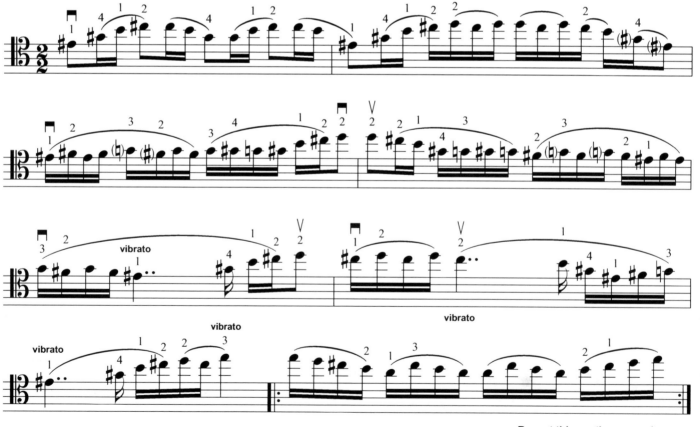

Repeat this section several times, playing faster each time.

Speed and Agility IV
Measures 448-450

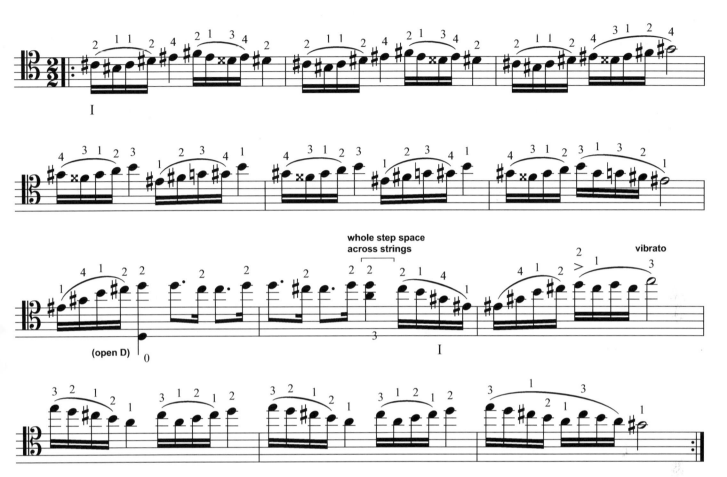

Repeat this exercise several
times, playing faster each time.

Rhythmic Shifting for Speed
Measure 449

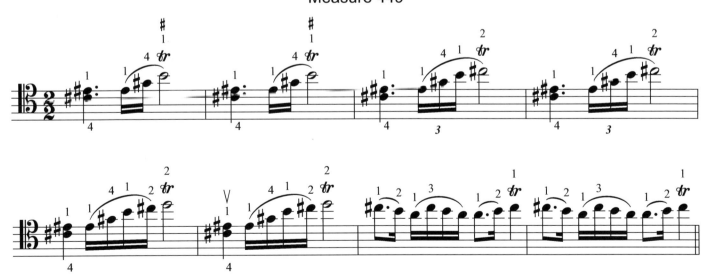

Transitions: Measures 450-451

Fluency: Measure 448-451

Concerto
Section Nineteen, Fingering No. 2: Measures 440-451

Learning the Notes I
Measure 440

Learning the Notes II
Measures 440-441

Note: In this exercise, only
the half steps are marked.

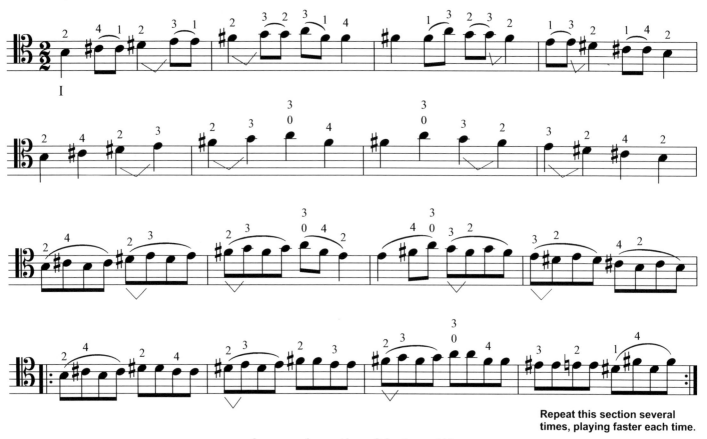

Repeat this section several
times, playing faster each time.

Learning the Notes III
Measure 440-441

Repeat this section several
times, playing faster each time.

Shifting to the Thumb I
Measure 441

Note: It will be more helpful to press the thumb down (no harmonic) in this section to help you learn spacing.

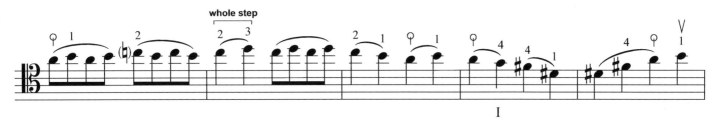

Shifting to the Thumb II
Measure 441

Repeat this section several times, playing faster each time.

Shifting Backwards: Measure 441

Agility I: Measures 441-442

Agility II
Measure 441

Repeat each section several times, playing faster each time.

Speed
Measure 441

Repeat this exercise several times, playing faster each time.

Speed and Agility I
Measure 441

Repeat this section several
times, playing faster each time.

Repeat this section several
times, playing faster each time.

Speed and Agility II
Measure 440-444

Repeat this exercise several
times, playing faster each time.

Speed and Agility III
Measure 440-444

Shifting Back to 2nd Finger: Measure 441

Learning the Distance from Thumb to First Finger: Measure 441

Shifting into Thumb Position: Measure 441

Speed and Agility IV: Measures 440-444

Speed and Agility V
Measures 440-444

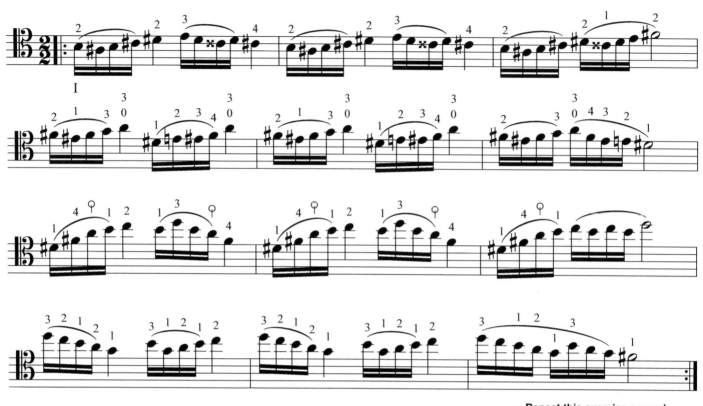

**Repeat this exercise several
times, playing faster each time.**

Fluency
Measures 440-444

Learning the Notes I
Measure 448

Learning the Notes II
Measure 448-449

Note: In this exercise, only the half steps are marked.

Learning the Notes III: Measure 448-449

Thumb Position Spacing I: Measures 449

Thumb Position Spacing II
Measure 449

Thumb Position Spacing III
Measure 449

Thumb Position Spacing IV
Measure 449

Shifting
Measure 449

Learning the Spaces: Measures 448-449

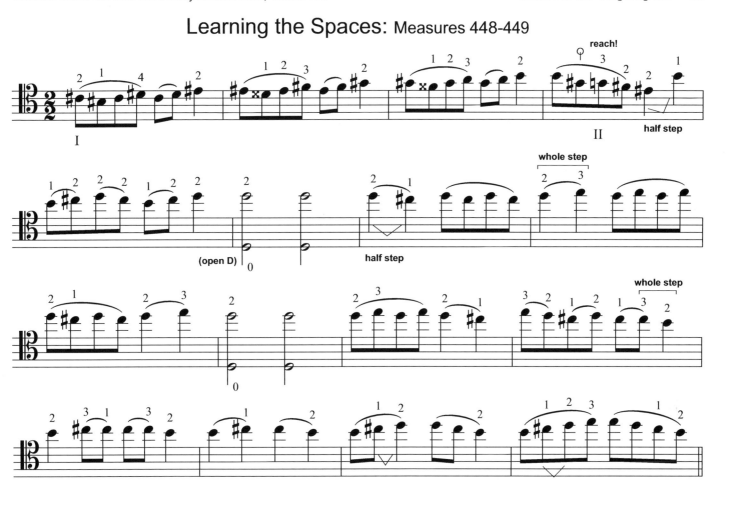

Learning the Notes I: Measure 450

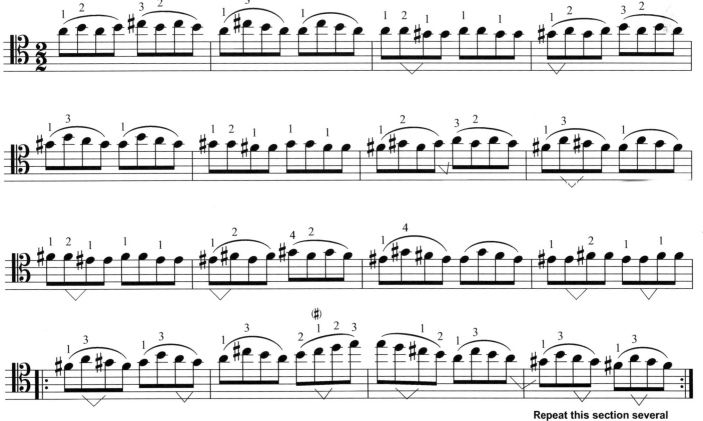

Repeat this section several times, playing faster each time.

Learning the Notes II: Measures 450-451

Spacing across Strings in Thumb Position I: Measure 449

Spacing across Strings II: Measures 448-449

Spacing across Strings III: Measures 448-449

Repeat this section several times, playing faster each time.

Speed and Agility I: Measures 448-449

Speed and Agility II: Measures 448-451

directly across

Repeat this exercise several
times, playing faster each time.

Speed and Agility III
Measures 448-451

Shifting Back to 2nd Finger
Measure 449

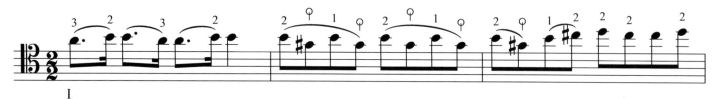

Building Muscle Memory for Spacing
Measures 448-449

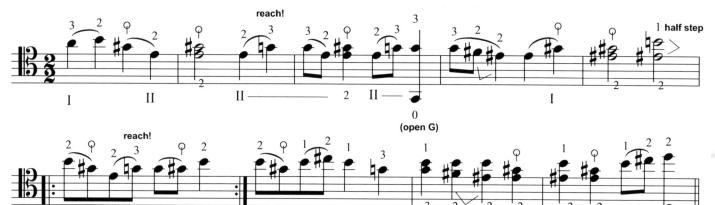

Speed and Agility IV
Measures 448-451

Speed and Agility V
Measures 448-451

half step

**Repeat this exercise several
times, playing faster each time.**

Fluency
Measures 448-451

Concerto
Section Twenty: Measures 452-468a

Shifting I
Measures 452-453, 456-457

Repeat this exercise several
times, playing faster each time.

Shifting II
Measure 453

half step   half step

whole step

Repeat this exercise several
times, playing faster each time.

Shifting III
Measure 457

Repeat this section several
times, playing faster each time.

Shifting IV
Measures 453, 457

Practicing Sixths with Half Step Shifts

Learning the Spacing inside the Sixths
Measures 454-455

Finger Spacing and Shifting Distance I
Measures 454-455

Finger Spacing and Shifting Distance II
Measures 454-455

Finger Spacing and Shifting Distance III
Measures 454-455

Finger Spacing and Shifting Distance IV
Measures 454-455

Mapping the Fingerboard: Measures 454-455

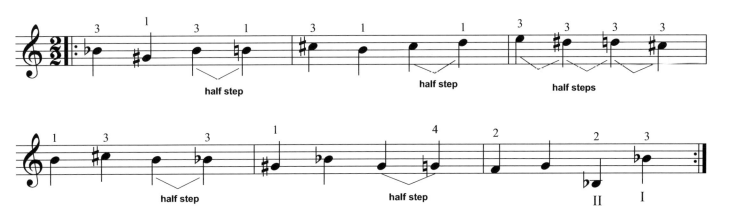

Crossing Strings and Shifting: Measures Measures 454-455

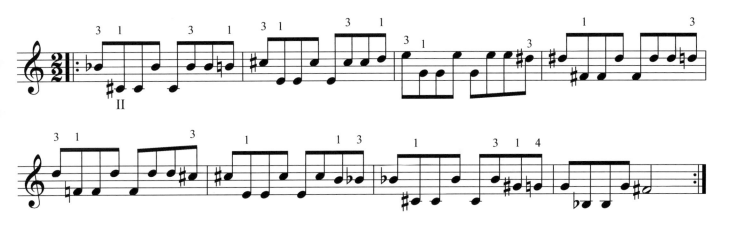

Bowing and Shifting: Measures 454-455

Getting into Position: Measures 454-455

Octaves across Strings: Measures 454-455

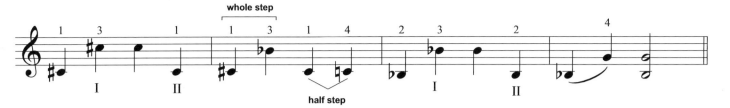

Learning the Distance with 3rd Finger I: Measures 454-455

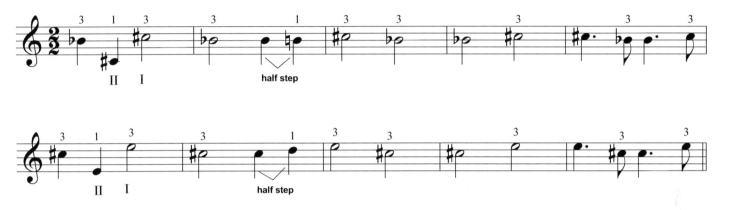

Learning the Distance with 3rd Finger II: Measures 454-455

More Third Finger Distance Training: Measures 454-455

Bigger Shifts: Measures 454-455

Double Stops for Intonation I: Measures 454-455

Double Stops for Intonation II: Measures 454-455

Connecting across Strings: Measures 457-458

Learning the Notes: Measure 458

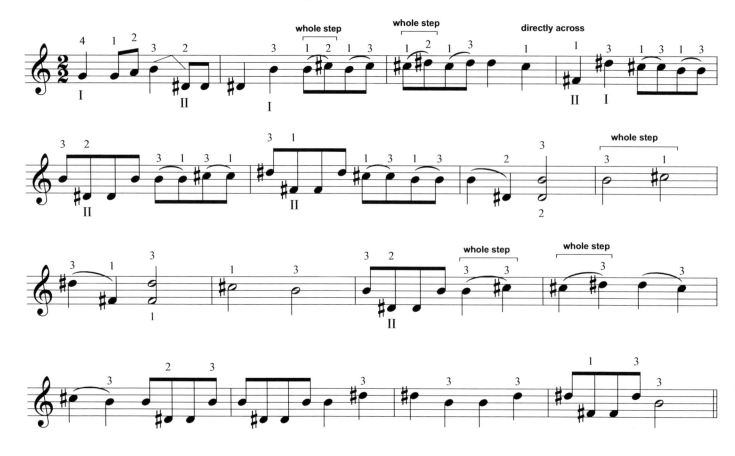

Learning the Spaces: Measures 458-60

Learning the Shifts I: Measures 458-460

Learning the Shifts II: Measures 458-460

Half Steps for Distance and Hearing Octaves across Strings
Measures 458-460

Fluency: Measures 458-460

Learning the Half Steps between the Notes: Measures 462-463

Learning the Larger Spaces I: Measures 462-463

Shifting with Third Finger I: Measures 462-463

Shifting with Third Finger II: Measures 462-463

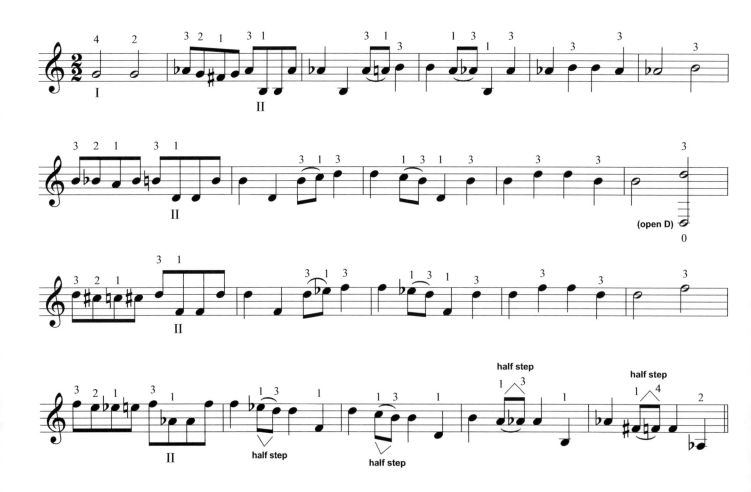

Hearing Octaves and Learning the Spaces
Measures 462-463

Fluency
Measures 462-466

Learning the Notes
Measures 465-468

Speed and Agility I
Measures 454-468

Repeat this section several times, playing faster each time.

Speed and Agility II
Measures 454-468

Speed and Agility III
Measures 454-468

Position Challenge
Measures 454-468

Repeat this exercise faster, accenting each note.

Concerto
Section Twenty-One: Measures 468-495

Learning the Shifts
Measures 468-470

Speed and Agility: Measures 471-472

Please note: some of the exercises in this section are deliberately awkward.
They do not have fingerings that are typical in cello playing but rather mirror the fingerings in the piece.
When played as fast as possible, they can increase fluency in the excerpt.

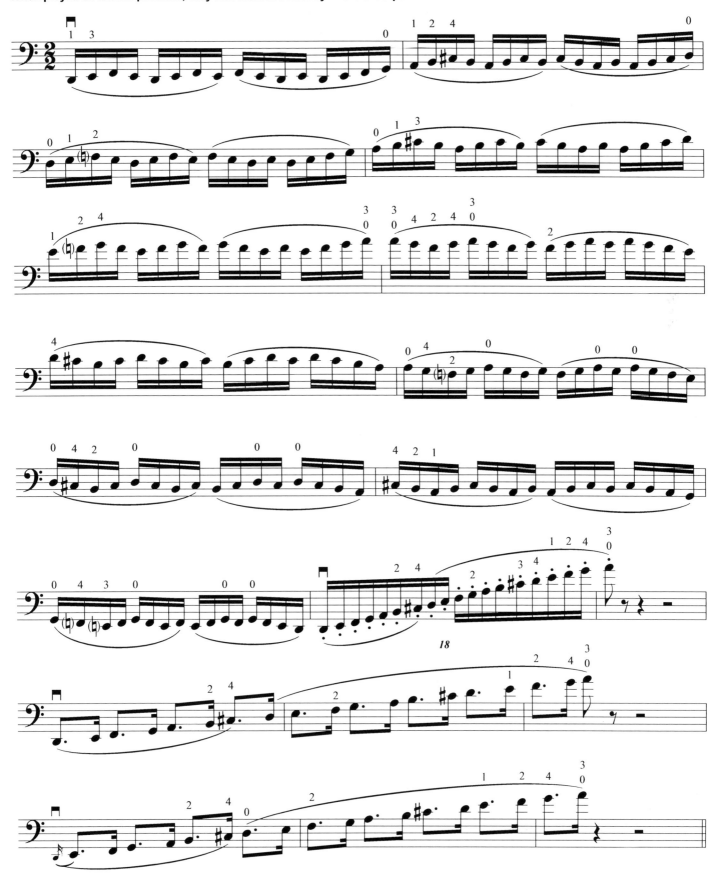

Shifting, *Top Fingering*: Measures 472-474

Shifting, *Bottom Fingering*: Measures 472-474

Speed and Agility: Measures 475-476

Note: This exercise is intentionally awkward to help the hand learn to navigate the shifts in the music.
After learning the notes, increase your speed to be slightly faster than feels comfortable.

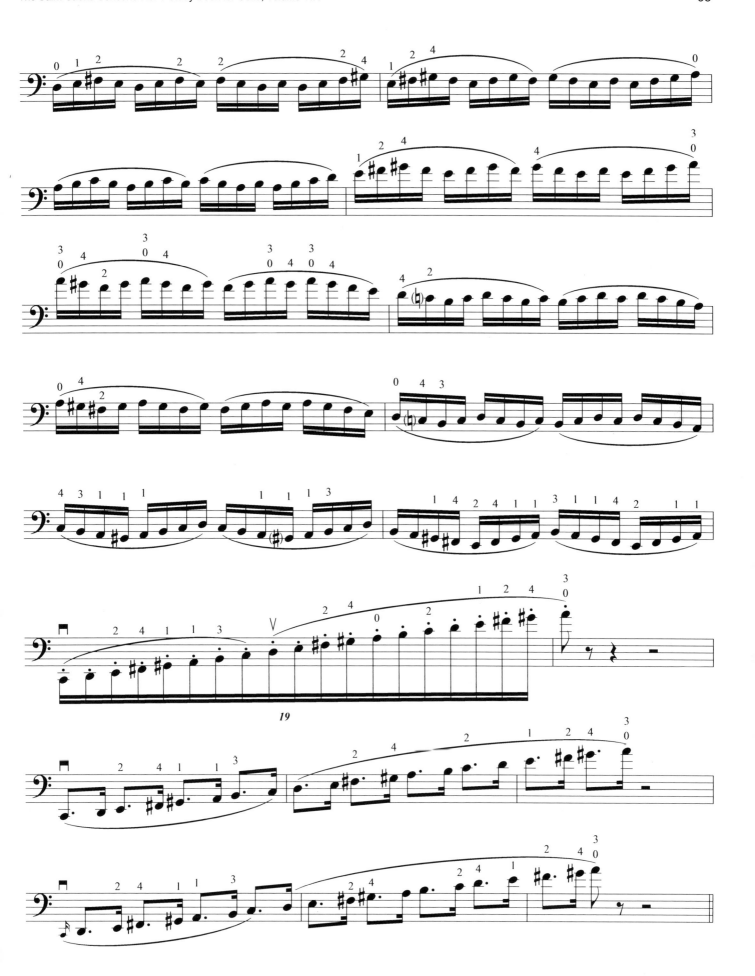

Preparing for Octaves I: Measures 476-477

Please note: In the following exercises, B♭ is used rather than A♯ to help readability.

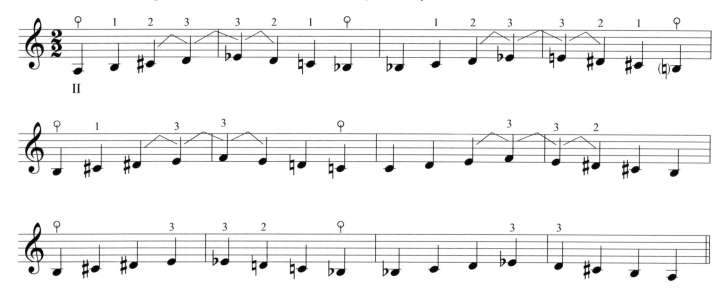

Preparing for Octaves II: Measures 476-477

Octaves I: Measures 476-477

Octaves II: Measures 476-477

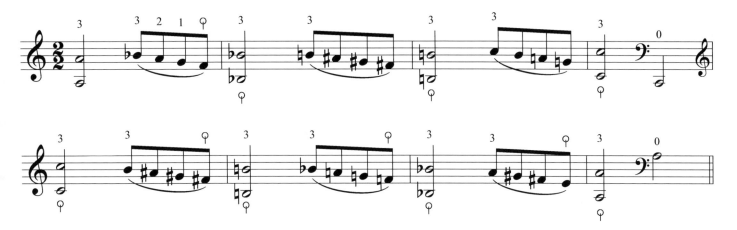

Octaves III: Measures 476-477

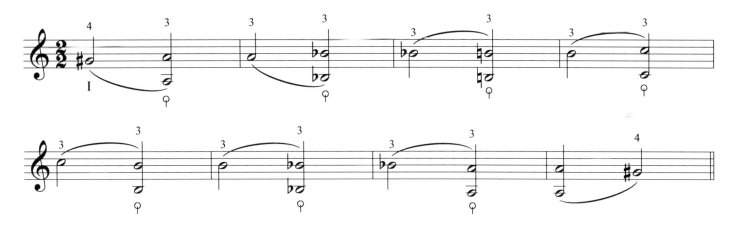

Octaves IV: Measures 476-477

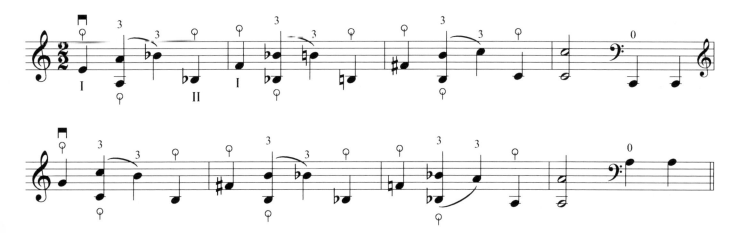

Octaves V: Measures 476-477

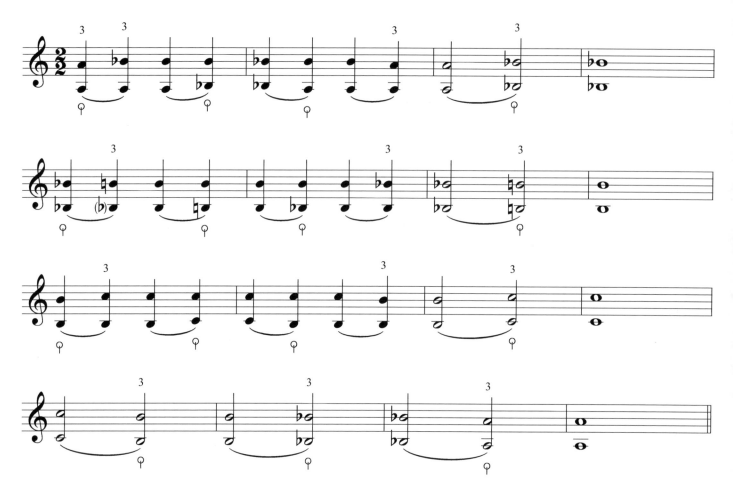

Octaves VI: Measures 476-477

Rhythmic Octaves: Measures 476-477

Shifting to the High F♯ I: Measure 478

Shifting to the High F♯ II: Measure 478

Learning the Lower Part of the Shift: Measure 478

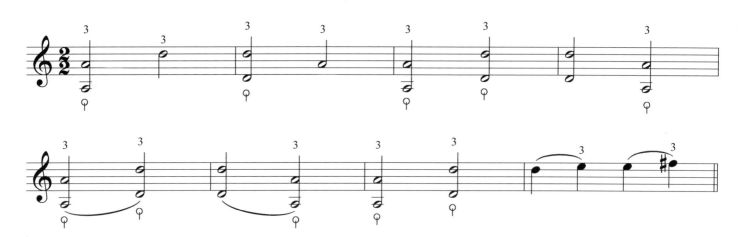

Learning the Upper Part of the Shift: Measure 478

Changing Hand Spacing as You Shift: Measure 478

Putting Both Parts of the Shift Together I: Measure 478

Putting Both Parts of the Shift Together II: Measure 478

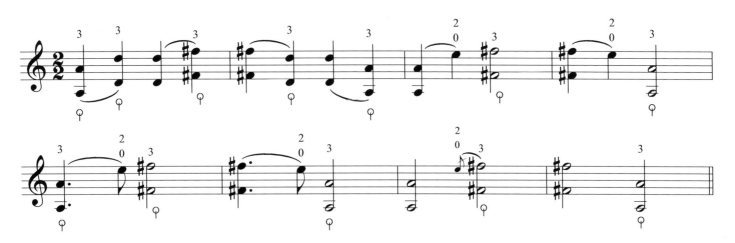

Shifting Back from F♯ I: Measure 479

Shifting Back from F♯ II: Measure 479

Accuracy in Octaves: Measure 479

Learning the Backwards Shifts: Measures 479-480

Putting it all Together I: Measures 479-480

Putting it all Together II: Measures 479-480

Putting it all Together III: Measures 476-480

Learning the Entrance: Measures 488-491

Concerto
Section Twenty-Two: Measures 496-517

Shifting: Measures 496-503

Fitting the Rhythm with the Accompaniment: Measures 504-507

Shifting: Measure 509

Fitting the Rhythm with the Accompaniment: Measures 508-517

Shifting: Measure 513, 515

Concerto
Section Twenty-Three: Measures 518-526

Learning the Notes: Measures 518-521

Learning the Notes: Measures 521-523

Using Shifting Notes to Find the Positions
Measures 520-523

Practicing the Shifts
Measures 520-523

Artificial Harmonic Notation in the Concerto: Measures 523-526

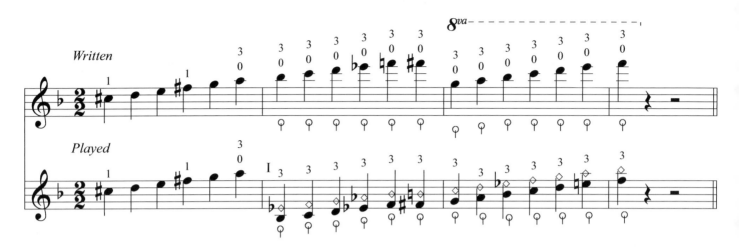

How to Play an Artificial Harmonic

half step

Press the thumb down on the string on the note F. Lightly place third finger on the string on the note B♭ as a harmonic (gently touch the string with third finger but do not press it down.) The first, second, and fourth fingers should be up in the air. While you are playing the harmonic, the thumb should stop the string completely.

Octaves as a Basis for the Harmonics: Measures 524-525

whole step

Shifting with 3rd Finger and Thumb: Measures 524-525 (middle part of run)

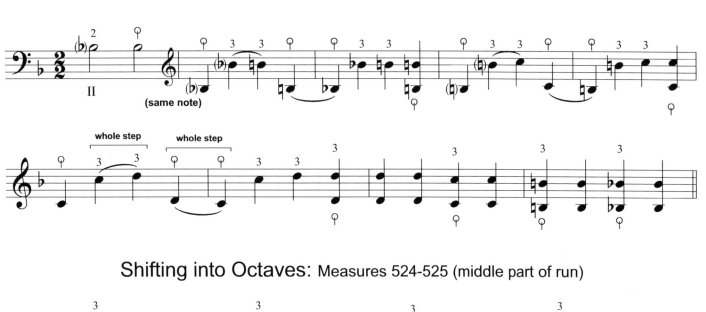

Shifting into Octaves: Measures 524-525 (middle part of run)

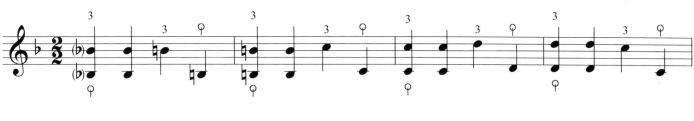

Artificial Harmonics I
Measures 524-525 (middle part of run)

Artificial Harmonics II: Measures 524-525 (middle part of run)

Artificial Harmonics III: Measures 524-525 (middle part of run)

Artificial Harmonics IV: Measures 524-525 (middle part of run)

Artificial Harmonics V: Measures 524-525 (middle part of run)

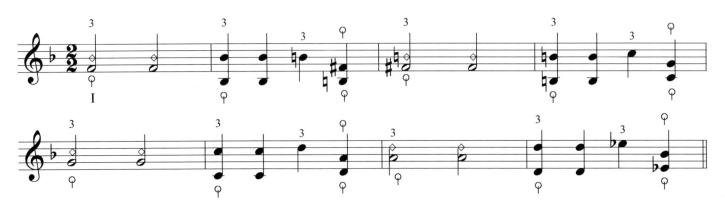

Artificial Harmonics VI: Measures 524-525 (middle part of run)

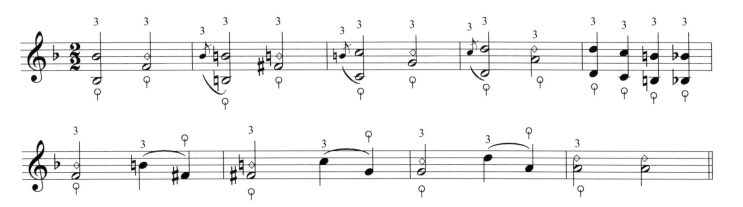

Artificial Harmonics VII: Measures 524-525 (middle part of run)

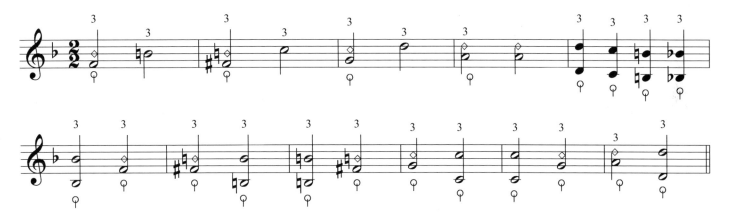

Shifting between Two Artificial Harmonics: Measures 524-525 (middle part of run)

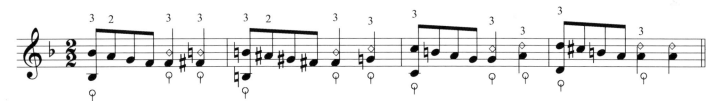

Learning the Octaves: Measure 524 (lowest part of run)

Shifting with 3rd Finger and Thumb: Measure 524 (lowest part of run)

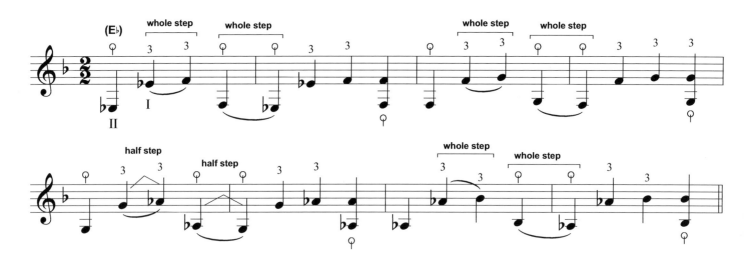

Shifting into Octaves: Measure 524 (lowest part of run)

Artificial Harmonics I: Measure 524 (lowest part of run)

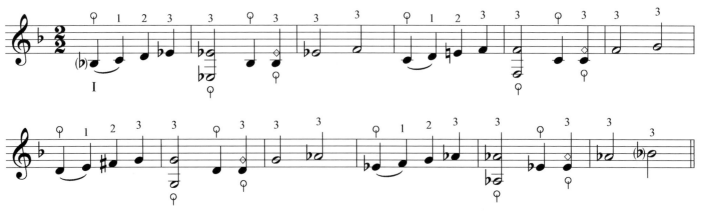

Artificial Harmonics II: Measure 524 (lowest part of run)

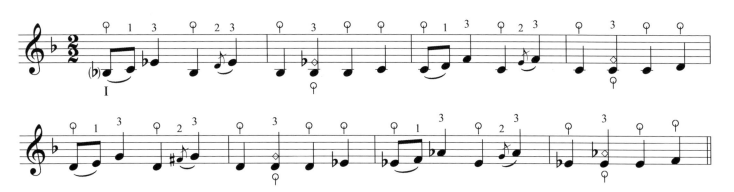

Artificial Harmonics III: Measure 524 (lowest part of run)

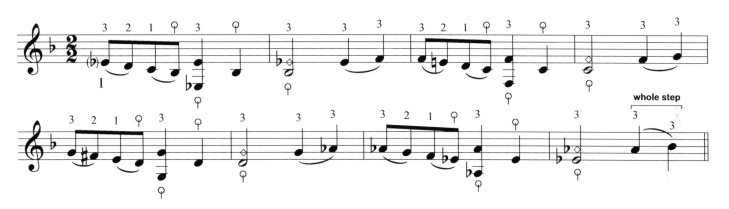

Artificial Harmonics IV: Measure 524 (lowest part of run)

Artificial Harmonics V: Measure 524 (lowest part of run)

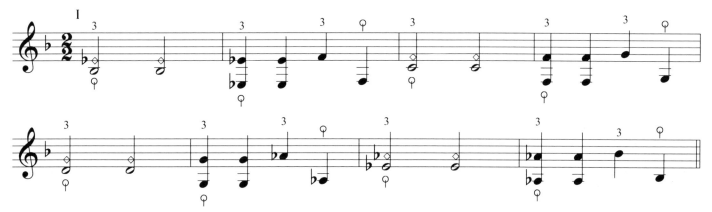

Artificial Harmonics VI: Measure 524 (lowest part of run)

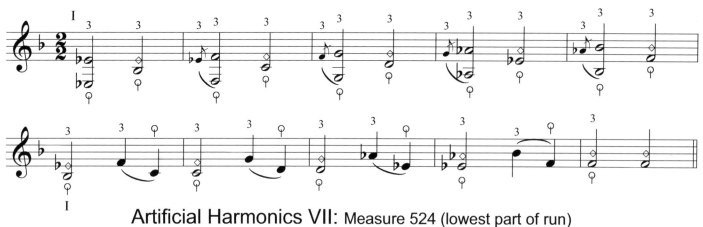

Artificial Harmonics VII: Measure 524 (lowest part of run)

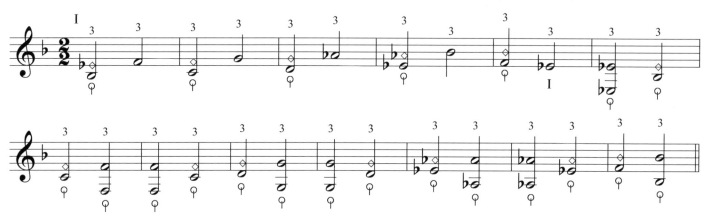

Shifting between Two Artificial Harmonics: Measure 524 (lowest part of run)

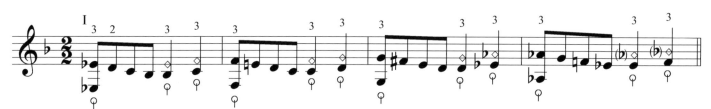

Learning the Octaves: Measures 525-526 (upper part of run)

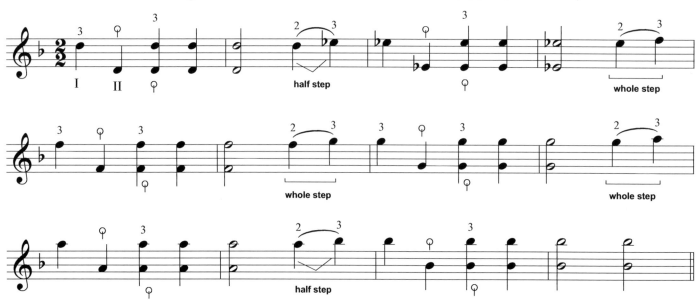

Shifting with 3rd Finger and Thumb: Measures 525-526 (upper part of run)

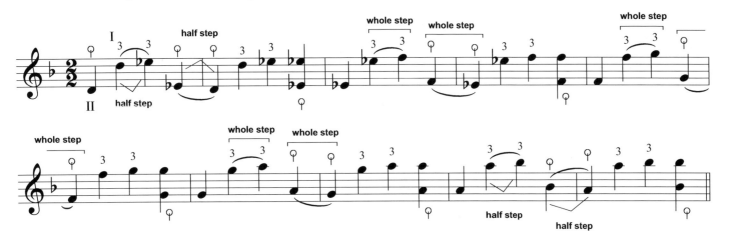

Shifting into Octaves: Measures 525-526 (upper part of run)

Artificial Harmonics I: Measures 525-526 (upper part of run)

Artificial Harmonics II: Measures 525-526 (upper part of run)

Artificial Harmonics III: Measures 525-526 (upper part of run)

Artificial Harmonics IV: Measures 525-526 (upper part of run)

Artificial Harmonics V: Measures 525-526 (upper part of run)

Artificial Harmonics VI: Measures 525-526 (upper part of run)

Artificial Harmonics VII: Measures 525-526 (upper part of run)

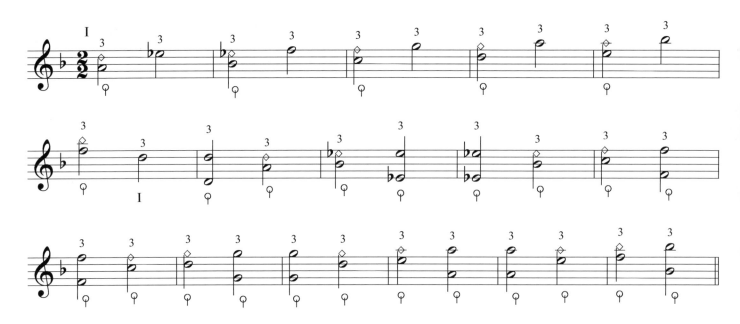

Shifting between Two Artificial Harmonics: Measures 525-526 (upper part of run)

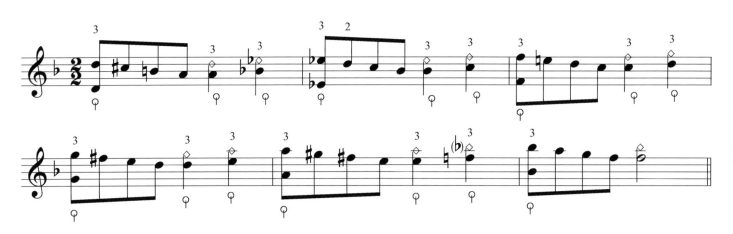

Starting the Artificial Harmonics after the High A
Measures 523-524

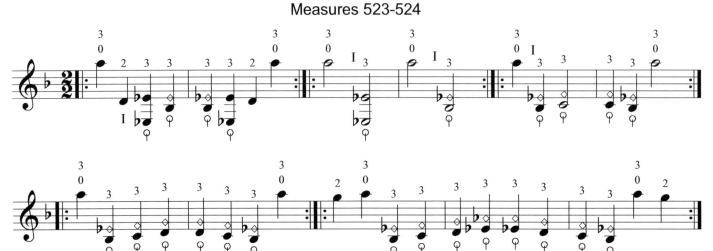

Mapping the Run: Measures 524-526

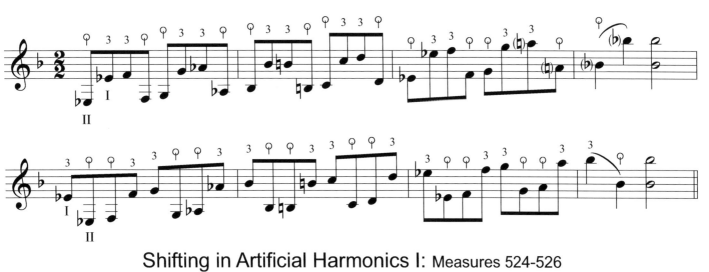

Shifting in Artificial Harmonics I: Measures 524-526

Octaves for Accurate Harmonics: Measures 524-526

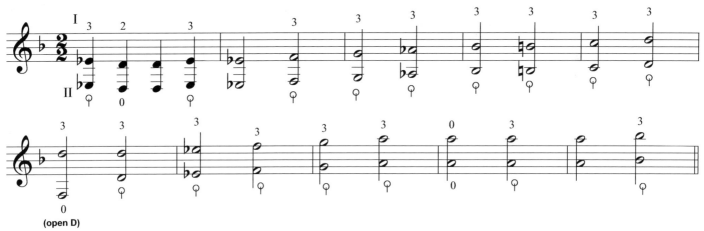

Shifting in Artificial Harmonics II: Measures 524-526

Using Octaves to Accurately Connect the Notes: Measures 523-526

Note: See page 155 for exercises on the *Ossia* notes.

Concerto
Section Twenty-Four: Measures 534-551

Agility and Intonation
Measures 534-535, 538-539

Practicing Sixths with Half Step Shifts
Measures 536-537, 540-541

Learning the Spacing inside the Sixths
Measures 536-537

Finger Spacing and Shifting Distance I
Measures 536-537

Finger Spacing and Shifting Distance II
Measures 536-537

Finger Spacing and Shifting Distance III
Measures 536-537

Finger Spacing and Shifting Distance IV
Measures 536-537

Getting into Position
Measures 536-537

Mapping the Fingerboard: Measures 536-537

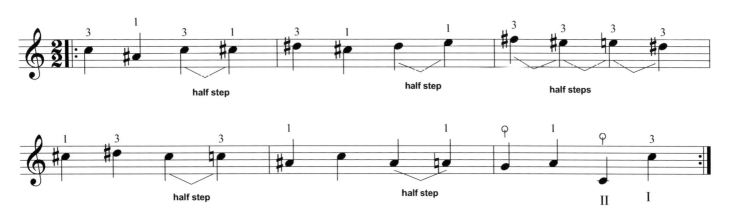

Crossing Strings and Shifting: Measures 536-537

Bowing and Shifting: Measures 536-537

Shifting in Half Steps
Measures 536-537

Learning the Distance with 3rd Finger I
Measures 536-537

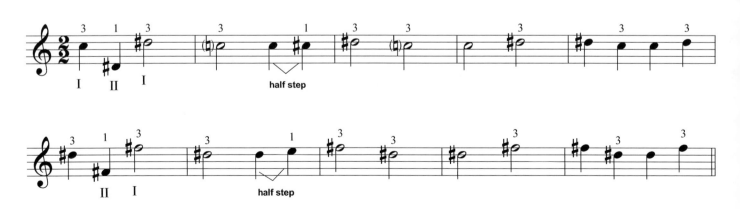

Learning the Distance with 3rd Finger I: Measures 536-537

More Third Finger Distance Training: Measures 536-537

Bigger Shifts
Measures 536-537

Double Stops for Intonation I
Measures 536-537

Double Stops for Intonation II
Measures 536-537

Finger Spacing and Shifting Distance I
Measures 540-541

Finger Spacing and Shifting Distance II: Measures 540-541

Shifting on Third Finger to Learn Distance I: Measures 540-541

Shifting on Third Finger to Learn Distance II: Measures 540-541

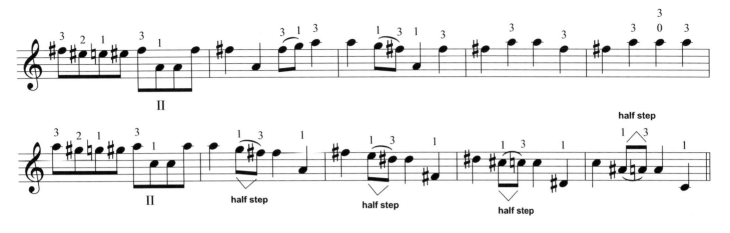

Bigger Shifts: Measures 540-541

Advanced Shifting: Measures 540-541

Agility
Measures 540-541

Learning the Shifts: Top Fingering
Measures 542--545

When using this fingering, all of
the shifts will be on half steps.

Learning the Notes: Top Fingering
Measures 542--545

Agility I: Top Fingering
Measures 542--545

Agility II: Top Fingering, Measures 542--545

Learning the Shifts: Bottom Fingering
Measures 542--545

When using this fingering, all of
the shifts will be with the first finger.

Practicing the Shifts: Bottom Fingering
Measures 542--545

Rhythmic Shifting: Bottom Fingering
Measures 542--545

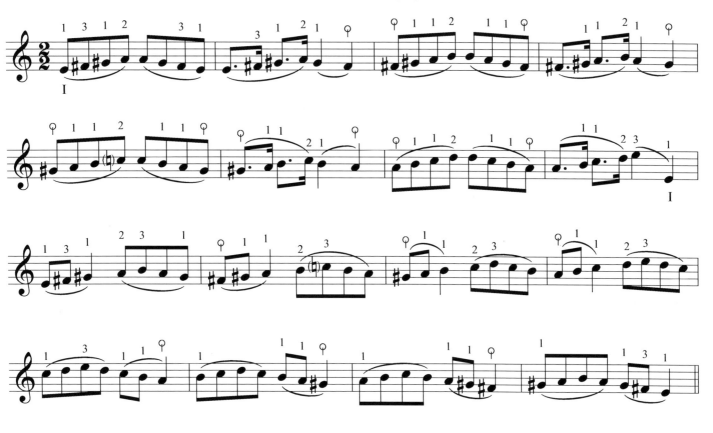

Agility I: Bottom Fingering
Measures 542--545

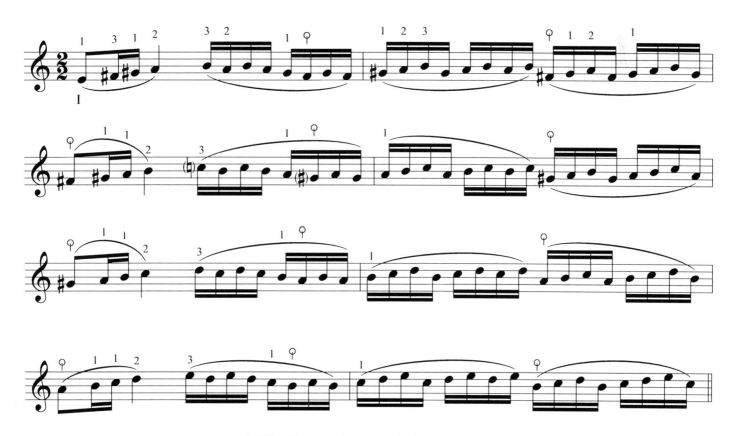

Agility II: Bottom Fingering, Measures 542--545

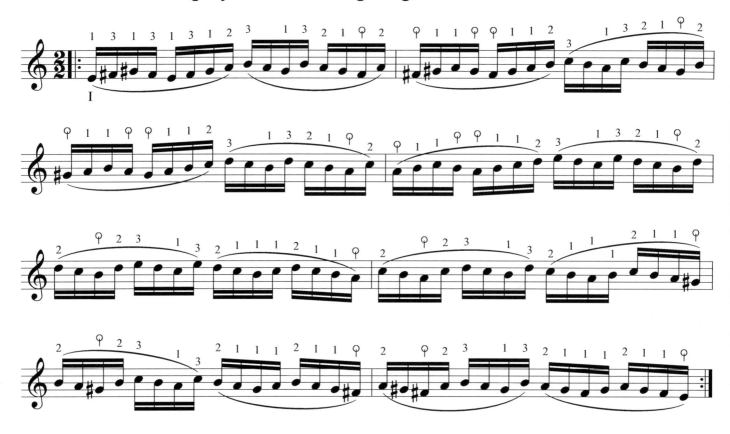

Holding the Thumb Down while Shifting to First Finger, Measures 545-546

Hold thumb on string for the rest of the exercise, moving only for the final note on this page.

Learning the Spacing, Measures 546-550

Shifting Backwards I, Measures 546-550

* = hold 3rd finger on string while thumb shifts to the next note.

Shifting Backwards II
Measures 546-550

Chromatic Shifting
Measures 549-551

Concerto

Section Twenty-Five: Measures 552-575
Exercises for this section are on page 17.

Concerto
Section Twenty-Six: Measures 612-end

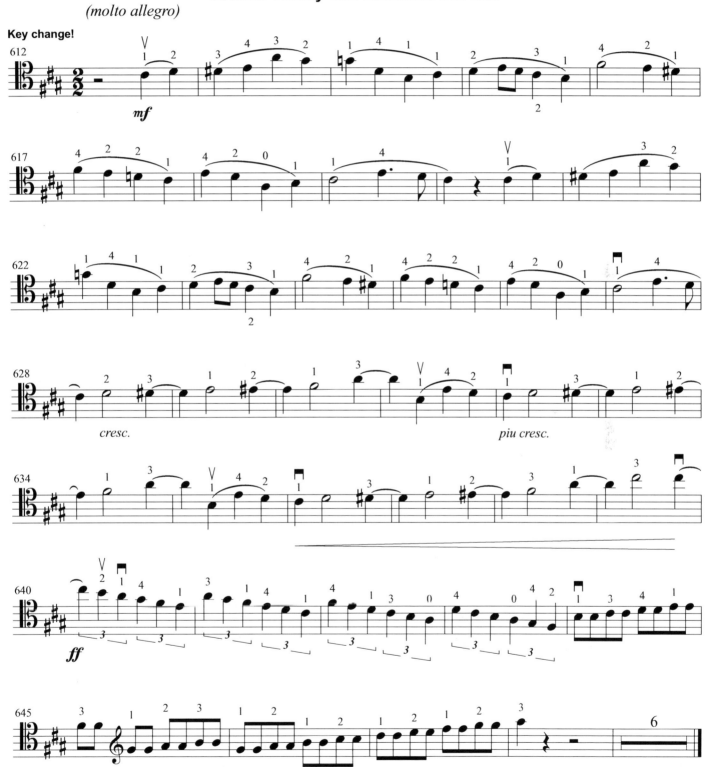

Shifting I: Measures 612-627

Shifting II: Measures 612-614

Shifting and Intonation: Measures 627-635

Learning the Notes: Measures 636-639

Intonation and Strength: Measures 636-639

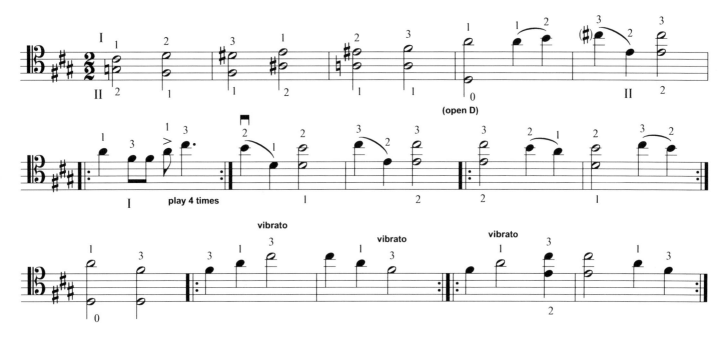

More Intonation and Strength: Measures 636-639

Learning to Play with the Accompaniment: Measures 627-639

Shifting Backwards: Measures 640-643

Finding the Positions Accurately: Measures 636-639

Learning the Notes: Measures 644-648

Practicing the Shifts: Measures 644-648

Connecting the Notes: Measures 644-648

Shifting I: Measures 644-648

Shifting II: Measures 644-648

Try to play vibrato on the double stops here.

Repeat this exercise several times, playing faster each time.

Shifting III: Measures 644-648

Repeat this exercise several times, playing faster each time.

Shifting IV: Measures 644-648

Shifting V: Measures 644-648

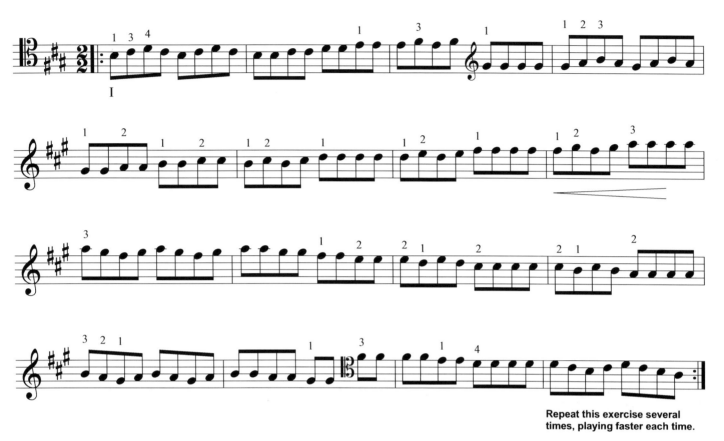

Repeat this exercise several times, playing faster each time.

Double Stops for Intonation and Strength I: Measures 644-648

Double Stops for Intonation and Strength II: Measures 644-648

Speed and Agility: Measures 644-648

Repeat this exercise several times, playing faster each time.

Addendum: Exercise I for *Ossia* measures, 521-526

Addendum: Exercise II for *Ossia* measures, 522-526

Addendum: Exercise III for *Ossia* measures, 522-526

Addendum: Exercise IV for *Ossia* measures, 522-526

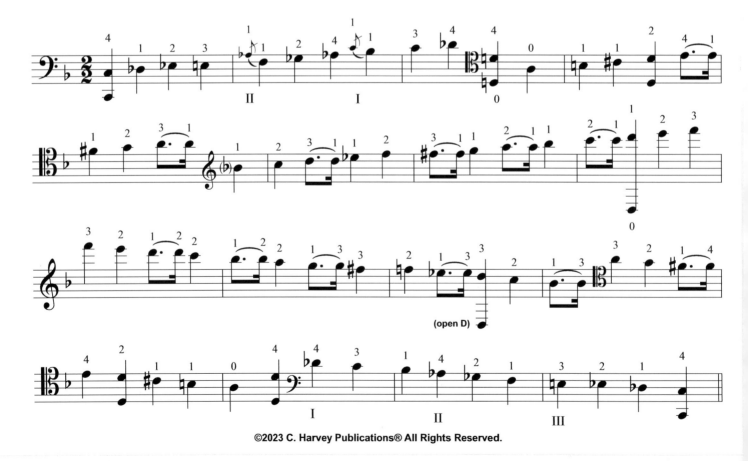

Concerto No. 1 (letter J to end)

edited by Cassia Harvey

Camille Saint-Saëns

Made in the USA
Las Vegas, NV
05 March 2024

86722449R00092